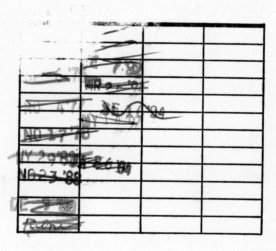

Contents

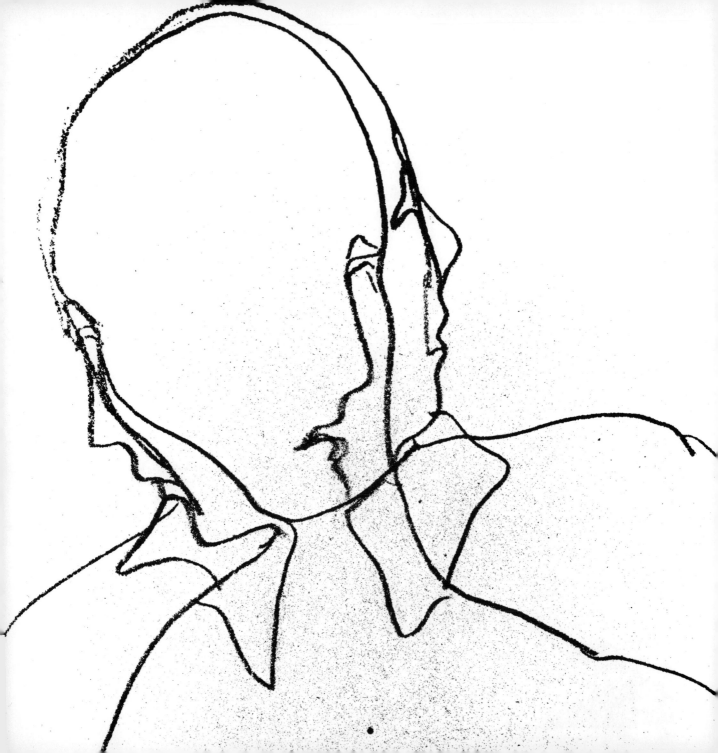

Introduction

Every time has a face. The basic tone of an era, its evolutions and revolutions, is mirrored in this face. Art is the messenger that carries the face through space and time in sculpture, painting, and crafts, from the marble head of an ancient god to the casual sketch of an anonymous human. The face may be that of a famous figure, perhaps Napoleon, who forced his physiognomy upon an era. More often the face is a timeless symbol: the classical Greek Stoic face, embodying the rational philosophy of a people; the Roman portrait, expressing the earthly power of the individual; or the smiling Buddha, revealing the eternal grace of religious authority.

Each moment in the history of man is recorded in the art of that time, and all of its art is finally condensed into the form of the face. The face is the organic link between form and source, the image formed on the wall as bits of time, art, and effort are scattered and scrawled across it. It slowly comes into focus, regardless of how many non-facial features are incorporated into it. Architecture and abstraction, design and crafts all finally come together with painting, sculpture, and all other arts to cast the image of the face for each age.

Sometimes a particular artist is identified with the face of an era (*Mona Lisa* by Leonardo da Vinci *is* the Renaissance). In so doing, he reveals, in addition to his own insight, all other artists of his time, a kind of creative synthesis. But more often the style created by the collective vision of all the artists of a period produces the historic form of the face.

This book asks the question: what is the face for our time? What style represents the contemporary face? When this is determined, to the extent that we are able to do so, we are left with the potential for directing students toward this face — naturally encouraging their own discoveries, but also showing them what has evolved thus far in the delineation of the contemporary face.

As expressed by the projects in this book, the contmporary face is the face rediscovered, the face shorn of emotions and sentiments, of fashion and polished forms. It is the face found in its parts, the dissection and reassembly of the parts to see what they are and what they suggest in new combinations. It is the face fragmented, like a puzzle that has no correct final image but is always in the process of becoming. This process itself

is also the contemporary face. Discoveries of new implications, discoveries of new contexts, discoveries of new patterns — in fact, discoveries themselves — are the impetus and the object of the effort.

The effort is accomplished by breaking down all the old forms. Early in contemporary art the features themselves were exaggerated or discarded. Polished geometric shapes of Brancusi's sculptures, distended features of Modigliani's heads, twisted parts of Picasso's work — noses, eyes, and mouths were reforged with the anvil of challenge.

When the challenge was heralded as a new reality, all contemporary artists felt the freedom to set their definitions of the face. It was exploded by Dali, squeezed by Giacometti, scratched by Marini, and otherwise altered into a thousand shapes. But giving every artist license to change the face to his will is not in itself a teaching method.

The teaching method on the following pages concerns itself with structuring the force for projecting the student into this new state of examination. This book is designed to build up this force for challenge — the love of the process of things — as the final quality that animates the contemporary face.

1.
The Face — Then and Now

The contemporary artist was thrust into his fascination with change by qualities peculiar to the modern world. It is a world of the machine: a time that takes things apart, reassembles the parts, and mindlessly mass-produces itself while another machine begins to take it apart again. It is also a world of codes, abbreviations, punched cards, and numbered lists. This is not exactly the kind of world sympathetic to the face of man. Yet man is the sum of his synthetic, as well as his natural, parts. And the artist in our complex journey through change is much like the artist during any epoch: both slave and master at the same time. He is mesmerized by the modern world, and yet he is able to challenge it. The challenge results in his continually changing the face so that the monolith can never identify itself, except for the quality of being always changing.

Faces of the past have had other qualities. Change was never one of them. Naturally they were different one from the other, and the transformation did not occur overnight. But they were always entering or leaving the state of a new face, never, like today, changing as a phenomenon in and of itself.

Some of the history of where and how the face has been is illustrated in this chapter. Like the multitudes of humanity they reflect, each face is at once clear and undefinable. To the extent that we can characterize each face we have an insight into that civilization. A compelling example: The Buddhist stone head on the facing page gazes out at us almost in a kind of frozen mockery. Its gentle face is a challenge to our understanding of the millions of people who adopted the philosophy of that smile. But we can at least see that it is a face of balanced, symmetrical forms with no small facial lines. The surface qualities are abstracted from everyday reality. Thus we perceive a culture turned inward and somehow in possession of calm.

Above. Egyptian Funerary Mask of
Hat-nufer, from Thebes; cartonnage.
(The Metropolitan Museum of Art,
Museum Excavations 1935-1936.)

Left. Greek Terra-cotta Head of a
Woman. (The Metropolitan Museum of
Art, Rogers Fund, 1923.)

The three ancient heads on this page and
page 8 touch upon a vast span of time and
attitude. The Egyptian face is locked into
an edifice of frontality. The hair, the ears,
and the eyes are set into a timeless pose
that allows for no individual response. In
contrast, the Greek woman seems to be
listening for every whisper and feeling
each new wind that blows through her
hair, and the Chinese Buddha on page 8
is desperately trying to reconcile his own
rugged physical nature with the subtleties
of thought scratched upon his face.

Opposite page

Portrait of an Ecclesiastic by Jean
Fouquet (ca. 1415/20-1481). Silverpoint
on paper. (The Metropolitan Museum of
Art, Rogers Fund and Exchange, 1949.)

Moving toward the present time, we see
a continued interest in the face as an
expression of the turmoil and anxiety of
man. Munch's face is filled with scrawled
shadows which run across his features and
imply a total impermanence of time or
instinct. The face by Giacometti is
trapped in white space which flows
through the drawing as if it had more
substance than the lines themselves.
Picasso has created the face of Balzac as a
race between each line which has its own
effect to make. In short, the contemporary
face is approaching us in the shifting form
of motion.

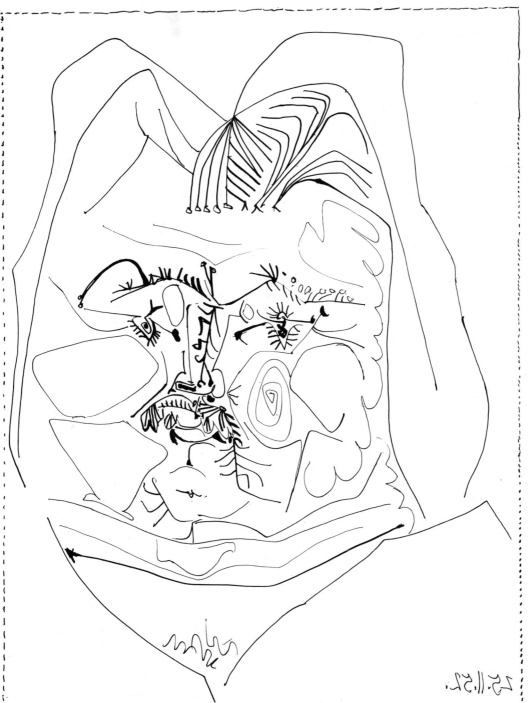

Head of Balzac by Pablo Picasso (1954). Lithograph. (Collection The Museum of Modern Art, New York. Purchase.)

These felt-tip drawings of faces by young children show the openness and vividness of their imagination. Their "play" with the face comes very naturally.

2.
Play with Faces

Fortunately, the contemporary artist has discovered the values inherent in the art of children. Their work has a natural, vivid quality that is often lacking in the more studied work of adults. In order to encourage our movement toward the contemporary face, it is an advantage to utilize some of the child's natural approaches.

These include the playful destruction of the image of the face. The child does this in his own way and for his own reasons, but the older student and artist can do it by literally cutting and tearing apart faces cut out from magazines. The ideal images would be photographs — rather than the artwork of others — in order to avoid the influence of a professional artist's personal style. By being broken up, the image immediately

becomes a kind of graphic play that releases some of the tension associated with doing the face. As reproductions in this chapter illustrate, when the pieces are put back together using the collage technique, the resulting puzzle suggests many new relationships which can be selected in preference to the standard eyes, nose, and mouth positions.

With this new impetus toward a free and relaxed approach, the faces can be created with bits of torn paper which may or may not have parts of the face from a photograph included. Amusing substitutions and juxtapositions can be encouraged, and the new faces that are formed will be the start of a healthy departure from the absolutes of traditional physiognomy.

The most practical way to structure

this approach in the classroom is for the teacher to select a variety of photographs from magazines. Most of the photos should be from advertisements or other straight, unstylized photos of faces. The selected pictures can be cut up in various ways. Some could be simply cut in half; others could have shapes (circles, squares) or features cut out. Along with the faces, a mixture of other images can be offered. These might include things also found in advertisements, such as parts of watches, gears and mechanisms of machines, diagrams, parts of maps, and other such mechanical or graphic material. The simple combination of these two elements — parts of the face and machine or graphic images — will immediately begin to produce a sense of play with the face.

The paper collages on these two pages
illustrate the range of possibilities this
medium offers. They go from the loose,
torn, free mixing of pieces and shapes to
the more studied placement of carefully
cut features. But all of the work utilizes
the advantage of being able to move
individual parts around until an
appropriate placement is determined.
Furthermore, there is no need to finalize
the work by gluing it down until many
changes are attempted, and each goes
through a metamorphosis from a
preliminary few pieces to the last, exactly
right selection.

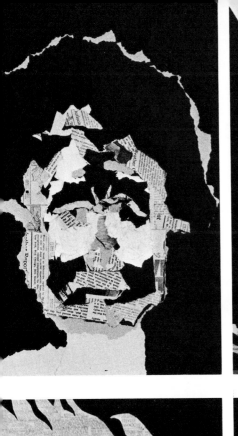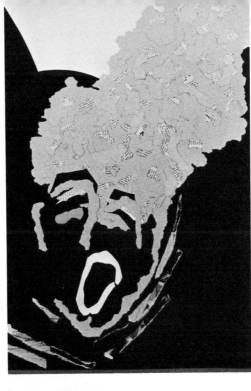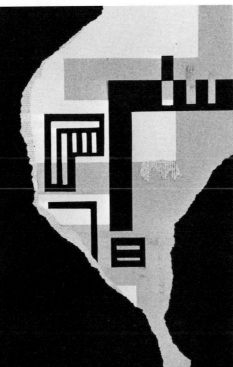

Finished example of first series.

Much of the fun of drawing over images is illustrated in these examples, in which the artist has cut up an image and then put it back together with his own lines made with felt-tip pen.

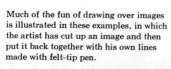

19

Both humor and exaggeration are healthy parts of the first efforts to reassemble cut-out images. As illustrated on these pages, every new combination makes its own statement.

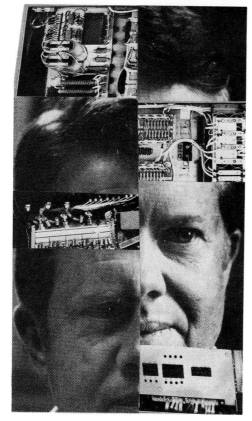

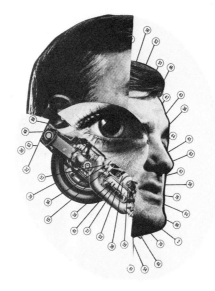

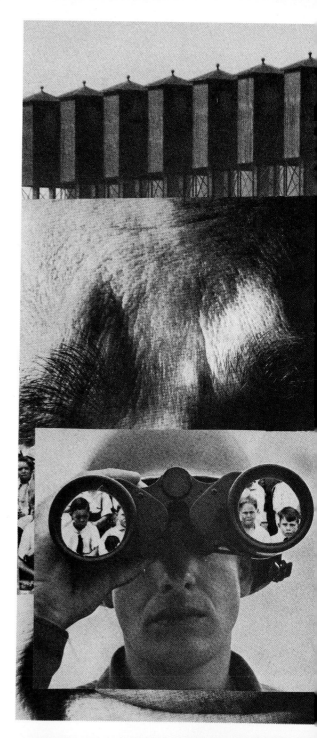

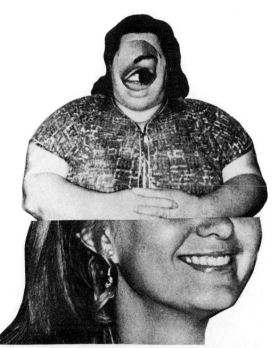

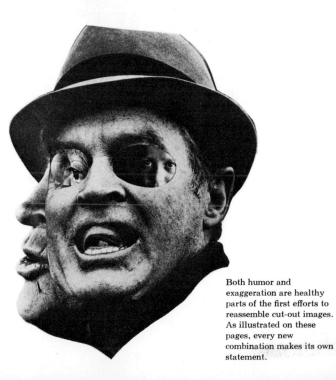

Both humor and
exaggeration are healthy
parts of the first efforts to
reassemble cut-out images.
As illustrated on these
pages, every new
combination makes its own
statement.

This face is an example
of the extension of the
photograph of a face into
a larger image. The photo
was cut apart, separated,
and then either repeated
or connected with pen,
pencil or watercolor.

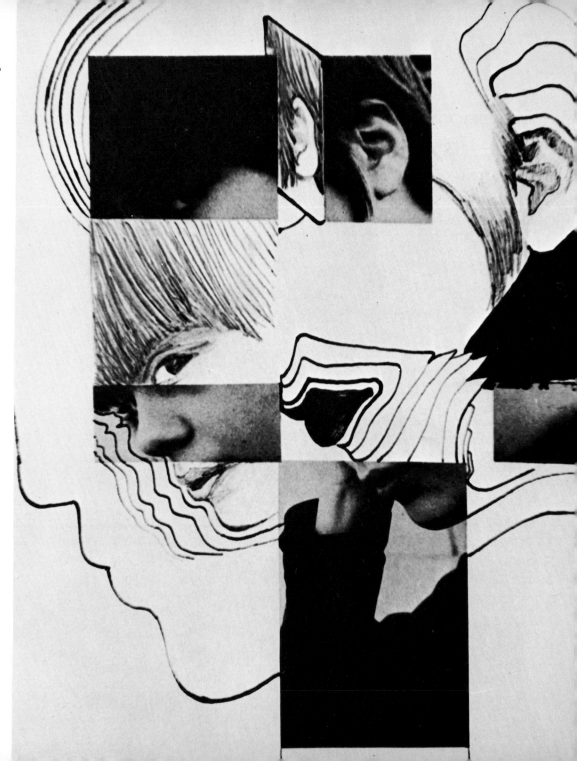

3.
Substitutions in the Face

The next step in the evolution of the contemporary face is the substitution of the artist's own concepts, images, and implications for part of the torn image he has been playing with. It is a simple matter of eliminating part of the ready image (the torn-up photograph) that he has been moving around the page, and replacing it with his own drawing. This may have already been attempted in the process of play with the face, and indeed it should continue much of the spirit of that approach. But now it can also include certain subtle techniques.

In this project, the face can be mirrored or repeated in a different spot or with different connotations. The line can draw out parts of the face and extend their meaning. As this intrusion of the artist's line upon the photograph continues, the fact of the face being broken up becomes less important, and the selection of lines becomes uppermost in significance.

The line is the signature or personality of the artist made visible and scrawled upon the abstraction of the torn face. The torn face thus becomes simply a part of the medium of the artist, a material — like his paints — with which he can create. He literally can begin work with a collection of torn parts of faces placed alongside his tools: brushes, glue, and other implements.

When a project is begun, the first step is to place the parts of faces down on a sheet of good drawing paper. Paper such as smooth bristol is best because it provides a good surface for the later addition of ink, pencil, colored marker or crayons. The parts of photographs of the face are placed generally no farther from each other than the space to be filled in with a drawing of the missing feature. Then, with a mixture of the materials — or a variation in the width or intensity of the stroke used — the missing features are drawn in. In many instances, these can be only partially finished in order to give a slightly unfinished character to the drawing, and the line can run over onto the photograph itself to complete the connection between it and the drawing inspired by it.

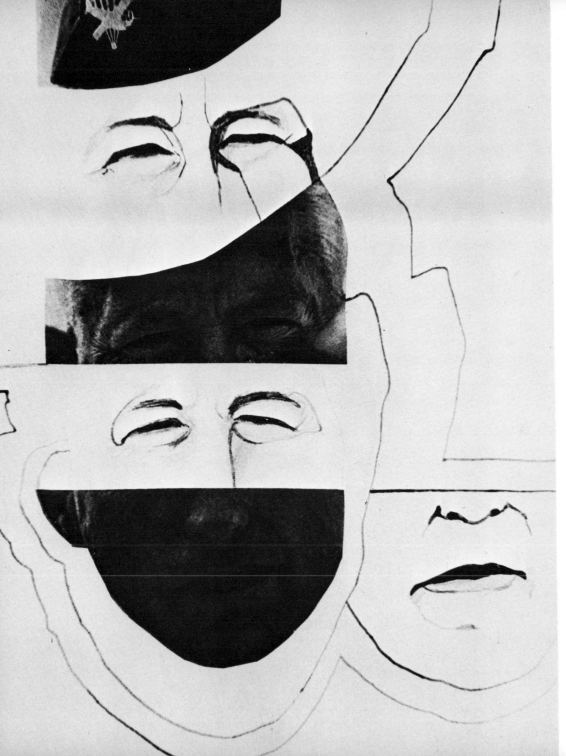

In these examples a single image was cut apart and became the starting point for an extension of itself by the addition of lines in ink and soft pencil. The result combines the qualities of reflection and sharpness of line as complementary elements.

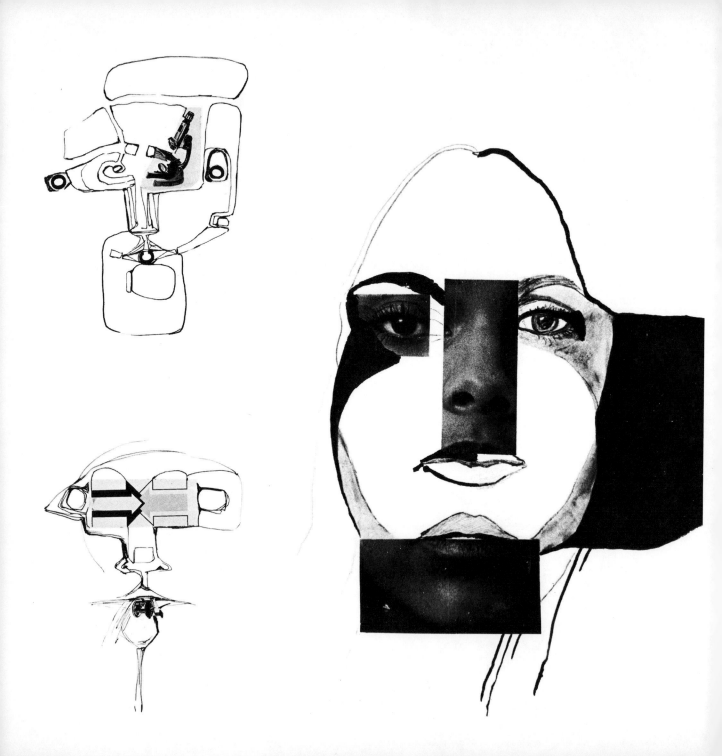

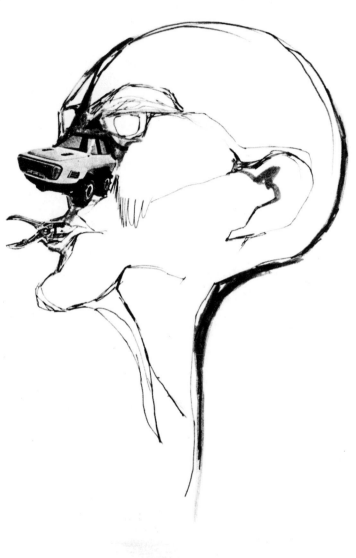

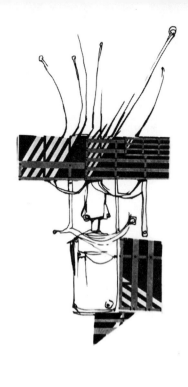

By taking a cut-out object and extending
it to become a face, the resultant image is
enriched by the peculiar character of the
object selected. Single cut-out objects
have been placed as central parts of a
face, then extended by adding lines drawn
with brush and tempera and felt pens. In
these examples, cut-out subjects as
diverse as pliers, cameras, arrows, and
autos have been transformed into parts of
faces. Occasionally the teacher can do a
"pilot" sample first to demonstrate the
project to a class.

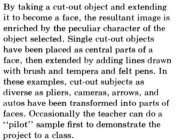

The sophistication of this approach combining collage and line can become quite refined. It is possible to extend some of the lines within the collage by continuing them as drawn lines — as in this example with felt pen and pencil — to create a back-and-forth relationship that gives the viewer pleasure in discerning what the actual image is and from what it is composed.

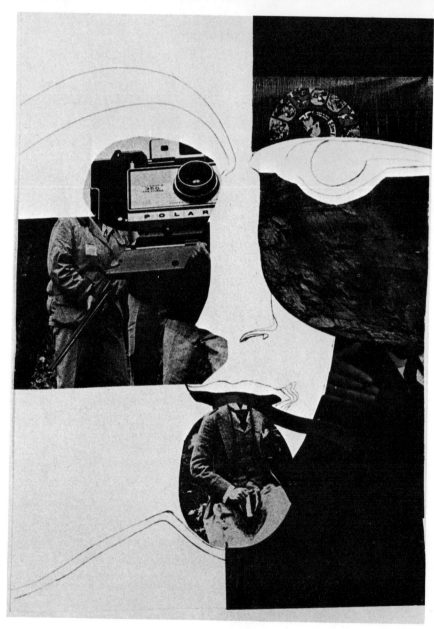

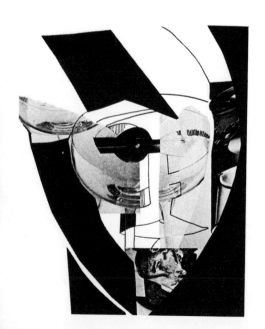

Some of these faces were composed from a series of photographs — all related to the same subject — collected from magazines. The connection between the images serves to make the face a representation of that subject.

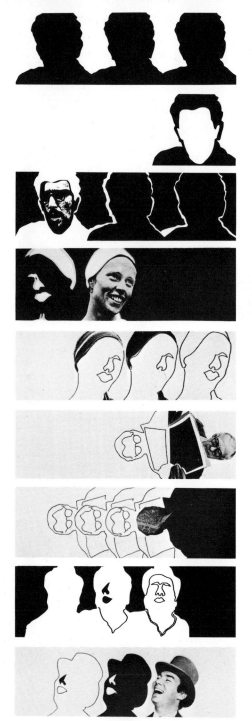

Each of these strips of faces made up of black and white papers and photographic details gives the same effect — namely, that the face on the strip has been repeated as if it had been stamped out by a machine. Yet the minor variations from face to face and the impact of repetition make each strip of faces more powerful than it would have been as a single larger face.

These sequences of photographs are composed of many faces of different sizes cut from newspapers and pasted together so that no black space is left visible.

4.
Multiplications of the Face

Sometimes the implications of the face are not readily apparent even with substitution and the play with its parts, demonstrated in the two preceding chapters. An approach that extends its range of meaning and also is very harmonious with the nature of contemporary life is the multiplication of the face. In this approach either the full face or individual shapes from the face are repeated many times in slightly different forms, or a face is subdivided into many small individual squares, and each part of the face is re-created in a slightly different way.

The effect of both of these multiplications (one being an outward and the other an inward multiplication) is to show that just by repetition of the same image, with only a small variation of form or style, the image takes on entirely new dimensions. It becomes a reflective judge upon itself. Each new step reflects upon the previous one, and they imply that many more alternatives are feasible. There is then an infinity of choices, and the role of the artist is again emphasized as being the selector of choices.

Each of these series of faces is a variation on the idea of multiplication of the face. The black-and-white patterns of the series above make it almost possible to read as a film script, with the characters reacting to each other, even though they are all the same face. In the other series the images look like the same actor changing his makeup from scene to scene. To create such projects, a photograph of a face is selected from a newspaper, cut out, and placed on black paper. The face is outlined on the paper with a pencil, and the new shape is cut out. This is repeated a number of times to produce several black paper cutouts. Then details of the photograph face (such as hair, mouth, and eyes) are cut away from the original and traced on the black paper cut-out heads. Each of these small tracings is cut out. This will produce a series of black cutouts with different parts of the face in white on each one. The original photograph details can now be added to some of the cutouts, and lines can be drawn on them if desired.

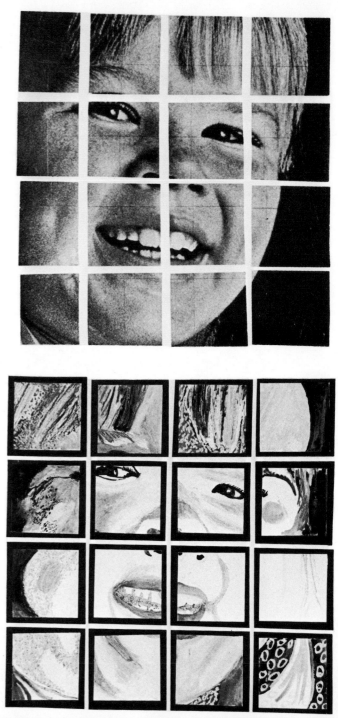

The faces above and to the right exemplify the process of cutting up a photograph and then reproducing it in new materials and shapes. These multiplications are done by taking a picture, cutting it into many squares, numbering each square, doing an interpretation of each square on a piece of paper (numbered correspondingly), and putting all the drawn squares back together in order of the original image. This allows for more variety than would likely occur if the original image were responded to directly. It is also a pleasure to see how each square relates (or fails to relate) to the squares near it. The finished examples to the far right and on the opposite page were created using the same technique.

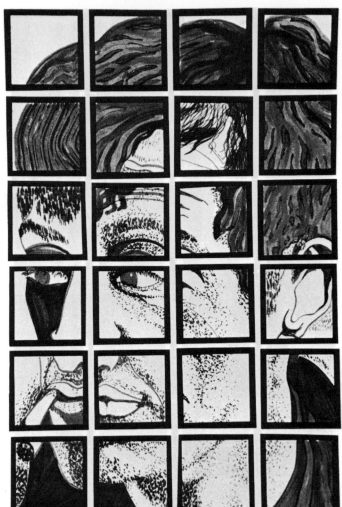
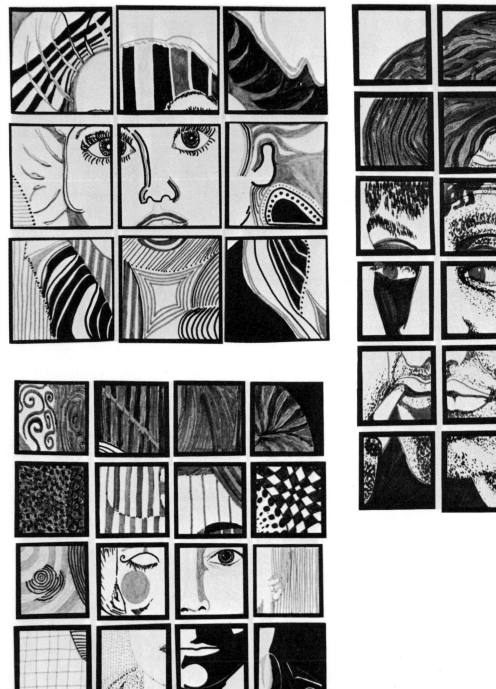

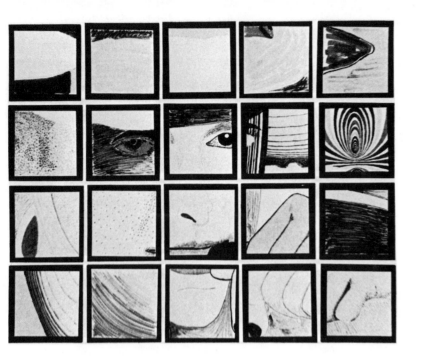

Many familiar images are transformed into new faces when done in this style of multiplication. The old image persists, clinging to its former lines, but the new forms delight in confounding the previous totality. The many examples on these two pages show this clearly.

This series increases its effect for several reasons. The number of faces in each square, the amount of line, and the introduction of new colors — all increasing in each subsequent square — tend to build up the impact of the sequence.

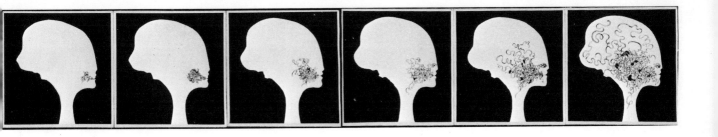

In this sequence the same-size, cut-out profile is used as a base for adding a pattern of twisting lines that come out of the mouth and gradually spread to the other features.

5.
The Face in Sequence

A corollary to the multiplication of the face is the sequential progression of the face. In this project not only can the face be repeated with slight variations, but it can build in progression within those changes. As the art in this chapter illustrates, the steps of change have a dominant theme, such as filling in the parts of the face, increasing the complexity of the details, adding color or shadow, or any other planned step-by-step development of the image of the face.

The idea of sequence itself in relation to the face is valuable because the face is an image that is part of the growth cycle. The calculated growth of the parts or style of the face directs attention toward the state of its self-fulfillment. Among all images, the face especially is perpetually becoming what it implies: older, stronger, more furrowed or

another related pattern. Thus, a face in sequence is following very closely the path of facial progression in nature. Of course, the artist does not have to choose the sequences of nature revealed in man's face. He can develop a sequence that is abstract or aesthetic or makes a personal commentary on nature's own sequences.

A face in sequence not only corresponds to the progression of nature as seen in the living face but also to the quality of programmed life common to our contemporary identity. Thus by sequencing the face, the artist combines the often contradictory paths of nature and the machine into the unity of a series of changes.

The best techniques for doing this sequential approach is to begin by cutting out a series of at least six squares of white paper (the minimum number required to create a sense of real change

from first to last step). Squares of about eight or ten inches are practical to utilize and later mount. Students should sketch with a variety of media, such as watercolor, ink, and felt pen, until they decide what they will choose to work with. At the same time they are experimenting with and thinking about materials, students should sketch a very rough sequence idea on cheap newsprint paper, using little detail. A general theme should be clear in the preliminary sequence sketches, such as getting closer to the face, increasing its detail or adding more color to it. When an idea looks promising, a student can begin his final sequence on the white squares with the materials he has chosen. Remember not to emphasize the realism of the face but rather the effect of the materials and the growth of the technique as it gradually effects the generalized image of a face.

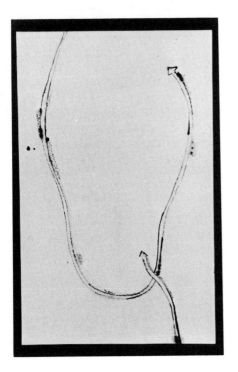
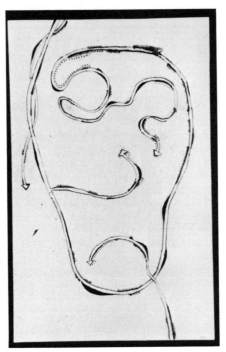

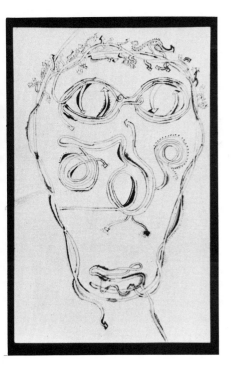  

These two sequences involve contrasting patterns of growth toward the completeness of the image of the face. The sequence composed of leaves grows to a balanced, natural image, while the other results in an unbalanced spectre of excess. In the first sequence, the student began by putting his chosen design motif, the leaf, in a random placement in one square. In each successive square he increased the number of leaves so that they progressively took the form of a face: gradually the leaves cluster about each area of a feature as more are added to complete the shapes of the features.

A sequence of the face becoming something implants in the viewer the realization that it might have become something else. There is no apparent absolute in the way the face progresses. Thus the face in sequence is only a momentary reality, soon to change and become another brief reality. In this problem the face was taken from a photograph (one photograph was given to each student). It was re-created in dots on separate sheets of paper, using colored felt pens. At first it was very lightly indicated with tiny dots; then each successive re-creation was done with heavier dots and more color.

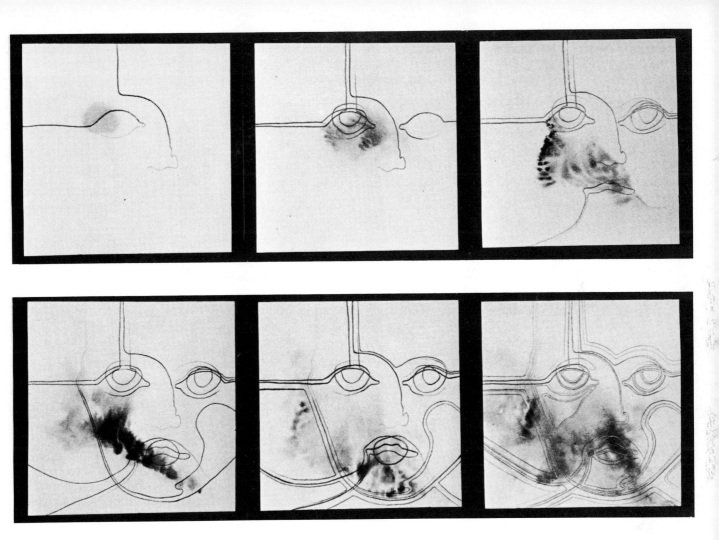

This sequence is a subtle
combination of washes of
color applied to wet paper
over which pencil lines
were later drawn. The
increase in the number of
lines slowly envelops the
soft watercolor washes.

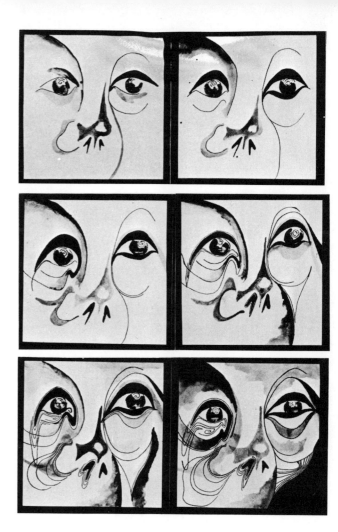

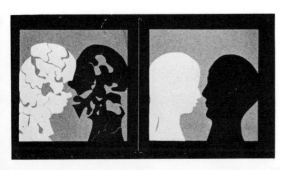

It is instructive, when we view sequences of the face, to compare the first image with the last. Naturally the contrast is greatest between the extremes and leads us to study the manner by which one extreme became its opposite: the jigsaw became an absolute, the sparse became elaborate, the anxious became neurotic. In the series at bottom left, two identical profiles of faces were traced on seven sheets each of black and white paper. Then each of them was cut up in the shapes of a picture puzzle and pasted down in increasingly exploded arrangements.

DON'T JUST STAND THERE,

ROBBED!

On these pages the faces are created from cut-out words. First, the words were selected and glued to the paper, and then the face was drawn about the words, reflecting their meaning.

6.
The Face Composed of Words

Words out of the mouths of men help to shape the faces that others see. It thus seems appropriate that words, phrases, numbers, and letters be used graphically to create the image of a face. This approach eliminates the step of making the words vocal by turning them into immediate images.

Besides giving shape to ideas and thus our concept of ourselves, words have many abstract qualities that can be utilized in the design of the face. When the design is related to the meaning of the words used, the potential for developing the face in new ways is extended even farther. For example, a phrase used to form the actual lips of a face could show the relationship between the literal meaning of the phrase and its use as an art medium. For ironic contrast it might be a negative phrase used to form a smile.

In this chapter words are used in a wide variety of ways, from a slight accent inside a normally delineated face to the whole fabric of the face itself. In each case the use of words allows the artist literally to "say" more with the face, and consequently to suggest more.

A practical method to begin this composition of the face is to cut out a number of words which could be key words for a face. Such words as "square" or "round" would indicate the way the face could be drawn. The words "angry" or "sad" would indicate the mood of the face. Then, one or more of the selected words is glued down on white bristol paper. It often works well if a word takes the place of a key feature such as an eye or the mouth. Next, the face is drawn around the word.

Another method is to cut out many words and then glue them over one another to build up the features of the face. Naturally, between the idea of the word expanded with drawing and many words combined without drawing there is a wide range of intermediate approaches. However, in all cases the essential aim is to let the cut-out word act as a start for the idea, a center of the image. The final face should be that word.

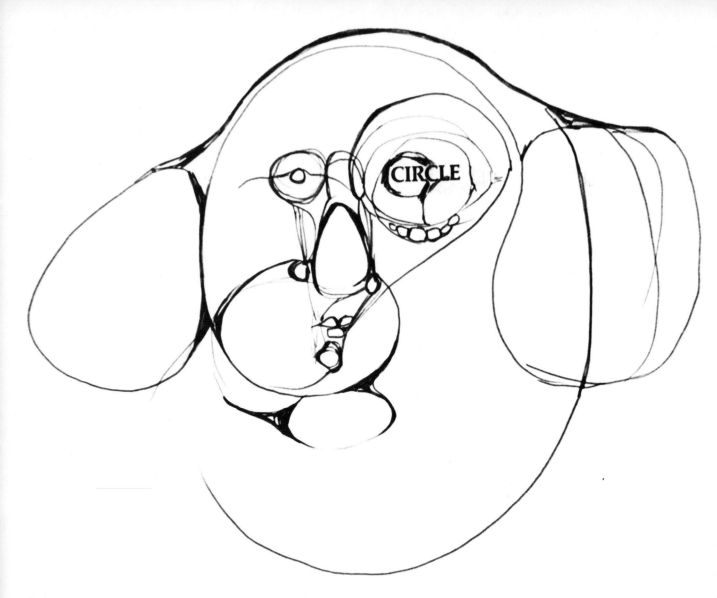

Words are incorporated
into the face in very
different ways. The use of
the word "circle" is a key
to the linear style used in
the drawing: circular lines
were used to create the
image.

48

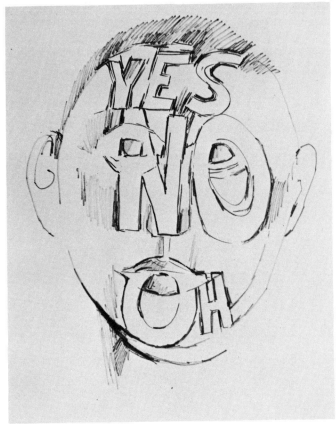

This face is a creation from the drawn word — "everyone" — split into two lines. The word is transformed as it becomes a natural part of the projection of the face.

In *Yes, No, Oh* and *Ever One* words are not pasted on but actually drawn and then incorporated into the faces.

The words pasted on these faces are a kind of narrative to be read with the form. They are whole phrases — or parts of phrases — that illuminate the character of the faces, which are finished with felt-pen lines attached to the photograph-letter fragments.

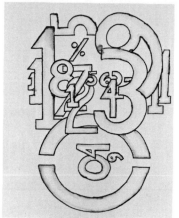

had run out

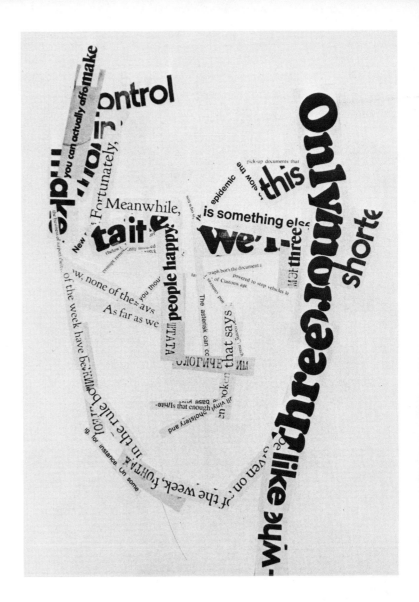

This assortment of faces using numbers, letters, and type cut from magazines, pictures with associated words, torn words, and words written and printed by hand gives some idea of the range of potential forms of the face that can be created with this approach. In some examples the face is barely perceptible, and part of our viewing satisfaction lies in discovering it. In others the face is very evident, and impact is stressed.

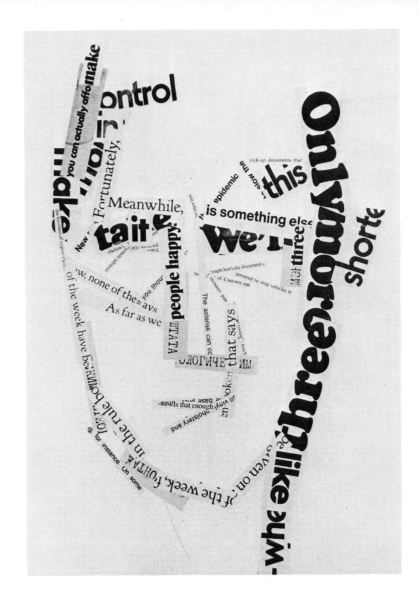

This assortment of faces using numbers, letters, and type cut from magazines, pictures with associated words, torn words, and words written and printed by hand gives some idea of the range of potential forms of the face that can be created with this approach. In some examples the face is barely perceptible, and part of our viewing satisfaction lies in discovering it. In others the face is very evident, and impact is stressed.

7.
Parts of the Face

Another inventive way to approach the face is to deal with its parts rather than with the whole cast of features. Alone or in combination with the others, each of the features can be depicted in a very independent manner. The artist need not concern himself with the relationships that normally predetermine the way he designs the features. He can let any feature by itself be a pure form separate from its relation to the rest of the face.

With this attitude it is possible, for example, to see the total expression of the face through the eye or to broaden the range of style used to define a given feature. In this chapter a variety of styles is used with various features in order to illustrate how easily the depiction of individual features lends itself to bold technique.

This experimentation with technique and parts of the face also tends to break down the contours, silhouettes, and oval forms so often welded to attempts to deal with the face. Now, flowing line or simply the absence of a definition of shape participates in the more open constructions of the face.

The best way to go about this project dealing with parts of the face is to start with the pen. In the classroom, use a drawing or lettering pen to demonstrate how it can be used in ways other than the normal manner. Turn it over so that it scratches irregularly, tap it so that it creates little marks, twist it from side to side to show curling line. Let the student experiment with the pen — not to draw anything in particular, only to try different effects until he finds the one he likes and can control. He should be able to make the effect go from light to dark by increasing its density and be able to extend it into a line, with emphasis on the effect rather than the actual line.

Then let the student take a new piece of paper and with a pencil draw lightly and very freely, with no detail, where he will place the feature or part of the face he wants to draw, and then draw that feature using only the new effect he has just mastered. The result will be a concentration on the effect instead of a concern for the realism of the feature. And, most important, the style will come out of the effect rather than from the student's limited capacity to draw the feature. Also, ironically, the result is improved if the student can draw with control and also if the student has a great deal of trouble drawing. In the first case the result will show an interesting combination of precision and technique, and in the latter case the technique will be heightened by its primitive application.

Each of these drawings is an expansion of a feature into a flowing form. The moving form implies a face but does not complete it, and, as seen on these pages, implies other possibilities of form without competing with them.

56

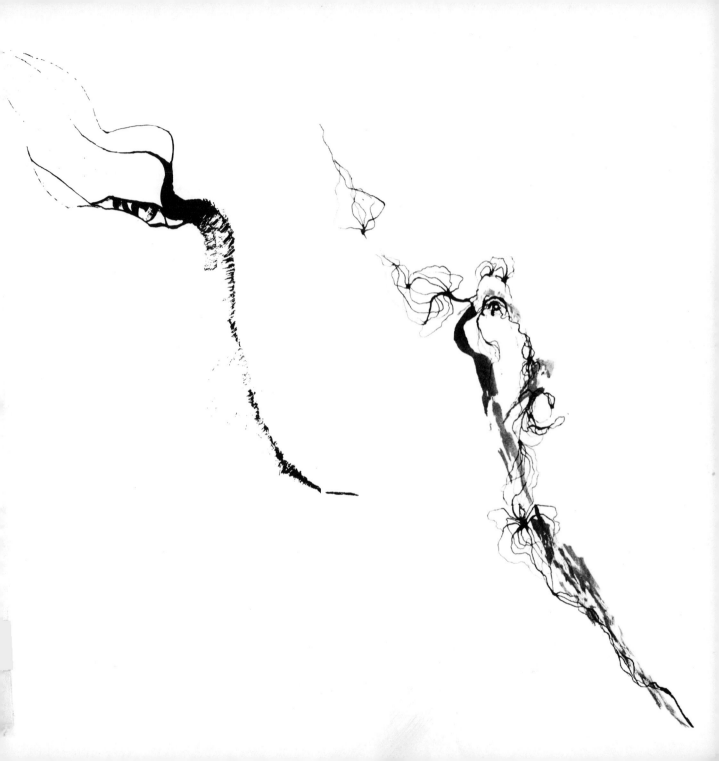

When concentrating on parts of the face, the whole spectrum of line can be applied. Dots, arrows, parallel lines, scratches, random flowing lines, all are potential sources for these studies. Sometimes whole faces are sensed from single parts, while in other cases it seems that the whole face is composed of only one feature.

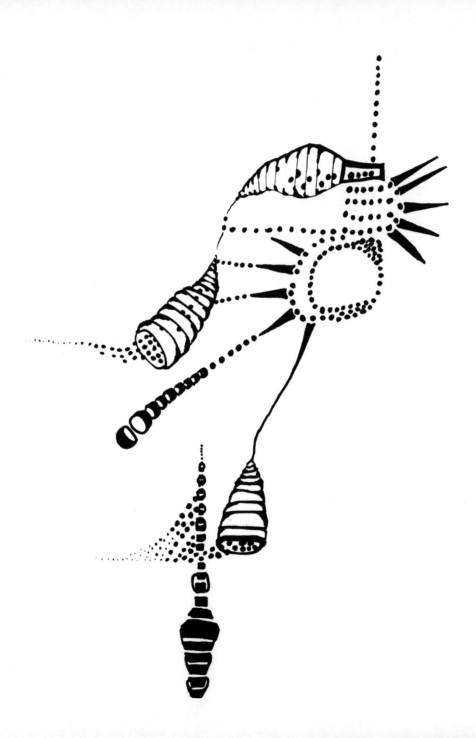

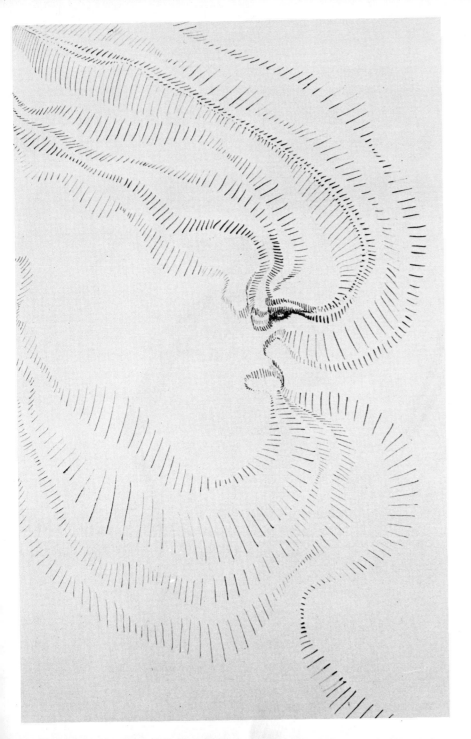

When the imagination is
fully developed with this
approach, marvelous
shapes pour forth. Who
would have thought to
make a feature out of
bones or to have them flow
from a wash, if the whole
round, complete face were
being depicted?

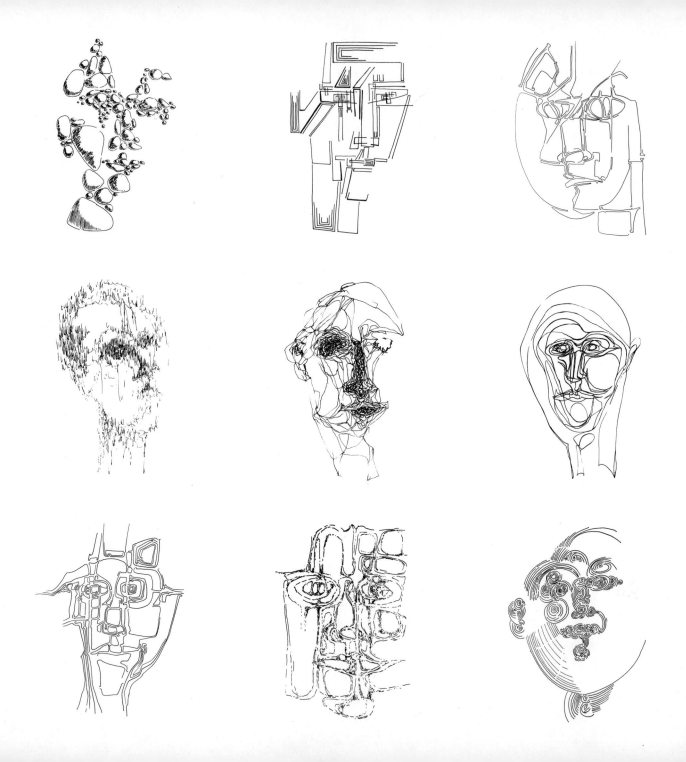

Opposite Page

Nine examples of faces
drawn with a variety of
techniques. Each style of
line creates a totally
different quality in the
face. Note that the shapes
of the features do not
reflect changes of tone so
much as changes of line.

8.
The Sense of the Face

Following the initiation of different techniques in conjunction with parts of the face in the preceding chapter, the next logical step is to extend these experiments with techniques to the whole face. This permits the technique to form the tone — or sense — of the face.

Often the artist tries to find in the face some indication of mood which he can use to give direction to his depiction. But just as frequent is the attempt by the artist to use a given technique alone to show the face. In this case it is the technique that seems to lead the form forward.

Acknowledging that this pattern is a valid learning approach, it is possible to stress the technique rather than the features or likeness of depiction. In this approach, all the student needs to concentrate on at first is his mastery over the sense of a technique and use its implications in creating anatomically generalized faces. A few rough indications of where the features are placed is enough to start the student who has practiced a technique on the face. Naturally, this procedure can grow into a more complete blending of the impetus of technique with the implications of the subject itself. In this chapter there are examples, particularly in pencil or ink, that demonstrate more clearly the point being made. They range from pure technique existing for its own sake to beautiful blendings of artist, technique, and subject.

In the examples reproduced here, a number of materials are used in addition to the pen. It may be useful to indicate some of the approaches that can be utilized with the other materials. In the case of pencil, use a dark soft pencil, and hold it very loosely. Make many soft, light lines all over and around the face, encouraging freedom and flow. Then encourage the student to select some of the light lines to make dark and strong. Another approach is to let students draw the face in the best way they can from life or a photograph and then take the point of an eraser and erase parts of the face with long back-and-forth strokes. It is best if they either erase quickly so that they have little control over what they erase or do it with their eyes closed. Then they should go back over parts of the remaining drawing with dark line. The point of these approaches with the pencil is to loosen the tightness and rigidity that usually occur when the face is drawn. Another idea is to use contour drawing and have a number of contours of the face drawn over each other. The use of colored pencils, crayons or felt-tip pens can be introduced on successive contours or after erasing part of the pencil work.

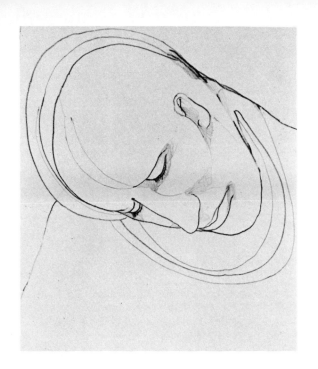

64

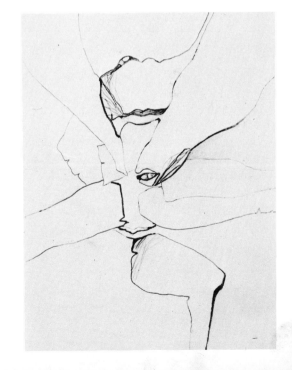

The principal medium of these faces is the pencil, and the techniques show how different strengths and pressures of the pencil produce variety of feeling. It is evident that by this time many of the qualities developed in the preceding projects are utilized in these drawings, such as stressing selected features, leaving parts incomplete, and repeating parts.

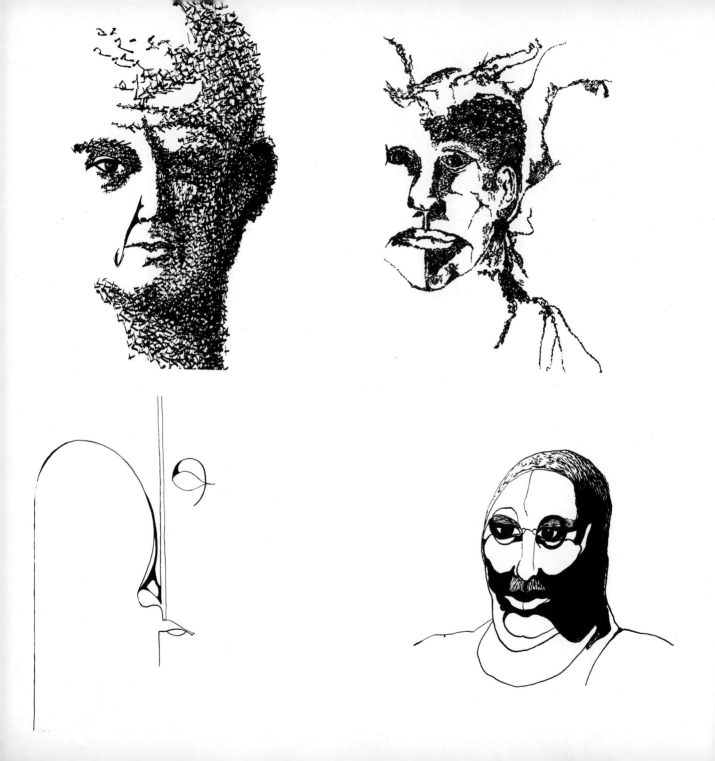

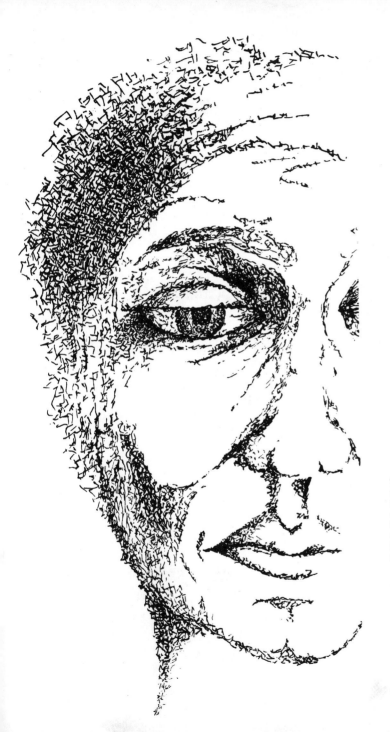

The best way to get the student to succeed with this approach is first to give him a technique. Then, when he has mastered some kind of line so that he can control it from light to dark and in concentrations of the line, let him apply it to a simplified facial sketch. The technique will add more than enough complexity to the face.

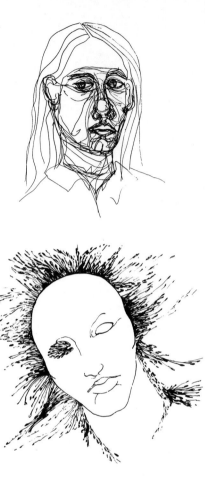

These faces, done first lightly in pencil to indicate vaguely the position of features and then worked out in technique, were all done by students who would not produce effective results if they proceeded by conventional steps. Their efforts would be defeated by their anxiety about anatomy, modeling, and proper depiction of shadow.

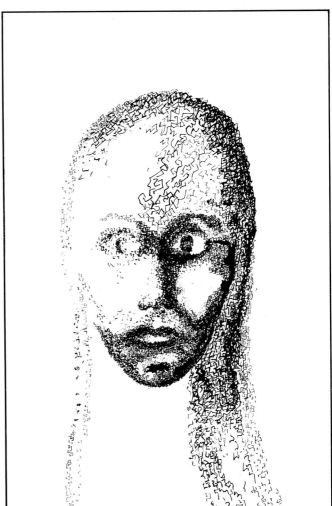

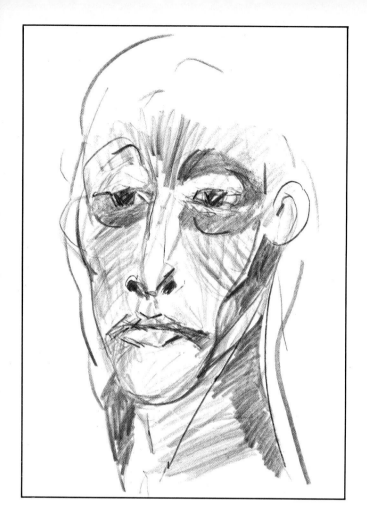

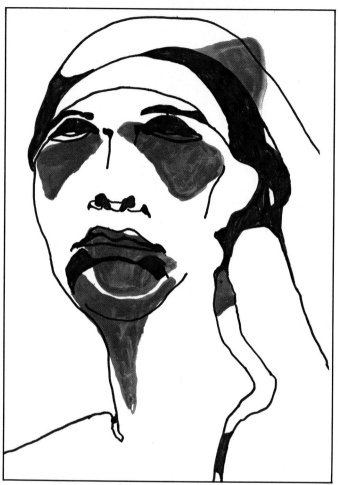

Technique with color, like that with line, can stress boldness or subtlety. These examples in color show those two extremes — one by using large, flat washes and the other by repeating many soft strokes of line. Any of these other faces in black and white could achieve some of the tones of color while still preserving their emphasis on technique by simply doing the technique in color.

The great variety of faces in the world deserves a variety of techniques to represent them. It is often techniques such as those on these pages which depend on unusual surfaces (dots, small circles, pen-point turned over and rubbed across the surface of the paper) that suggest this variety in faces most effectively.

Above on this page are the
original examples of layers
of art for creating a face by
layers.

9.
Layers of the Face

The face is a many-layered form. Each change of expression, light, mood, and time in turn gives a different cast to the face. Yet few ways of depicting the face allows for these changes.

One way to begin to suggest this growth of layers of form interacting is literally to compose the face by using transparent materials. Many layers of plastic sheets or tissue paper can be used together with opaque materials. Inks or cut-out forms on the plastic sheets each represent one layer of the face. Then the viewer of the finished work can follow the development of the face either by placing one layer over the other, or he may choose to combine different layers in any order of his own preference.

Obviously, if layers that are sufficiently different from one another are used, the viewer of the image can combine the layers in a variety of ways to form very contrasting faces. He could also include color or other refinements to alter the effect.

The practical way to approach the layering of the face is first to cut up equal-size squares of clear acetate plastic. It is best to use flat sheets of plastic rather than rolls, as the rolls tend to curl. Also work with plastic in as heavy a weight as you can afford. The heavier it is, the better it stays flat, can be worked with, and can be moved around for change in the combinations of the face. Then cut or draw a face to fit within the square of plastic and place it on the plastic. Now put another square of the plastic over the first, and you are ready to start. On this second sheet of plastic you may use acetate (which doesn't crawl on plastic) and magic markers or glue on bits of construction paper or other images. Try with each successive layer of plastic to leave part of the face and plastic clear so that at least one or more of the other images on plastic beneath it can be seen. As you work, occasionally move one or more of the bottom layers out to see how it looks over the layer you are now doing on top. Keep interchanging the layers until you have a number that can be combined with different results. Some should have very little on them — perhaps just one feature and a contour of the face. Others might have most of the face masked out in construction paper with only small parts cut out to see through. Remember that any two plastic squares placed on top of each other and then reversed will have very different effects.

These faces are composed by putting some detail of the face on different layers (first three acetate, bottom layer white paper) and then building up the layers until the whole face is fulfilled. The interesting aspect is how complete in its own way each combination is, even without the other layers added.

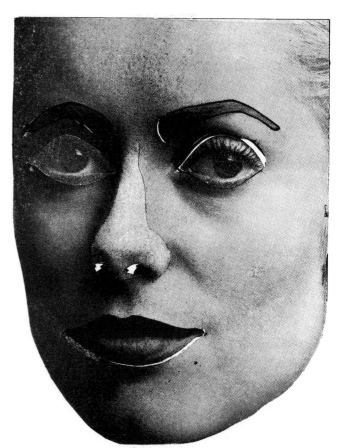

The two series illustrate varied
layer combinations of the
layers that form the two faces on
the opposite page. *Top row* (left face):
1. bottom and second layers. 2. bottom
layer alone. 3. second layer alone.
Lower row (right face): 1. bottom and
second layers. 2. bottom layer alone.
3. second layer alone.

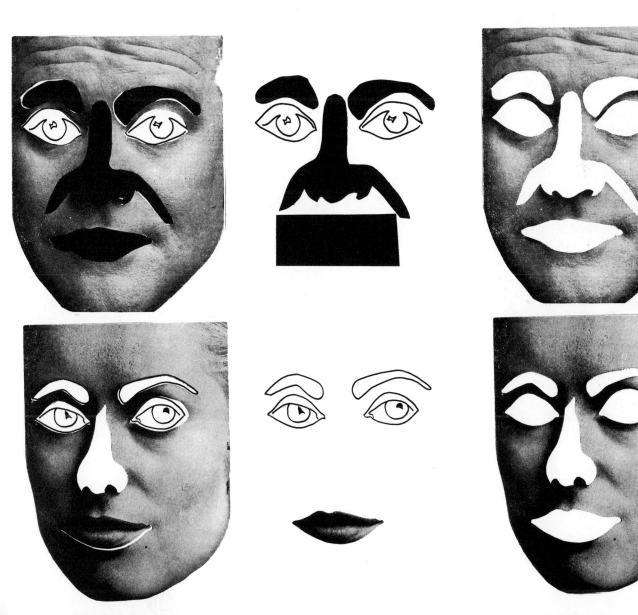

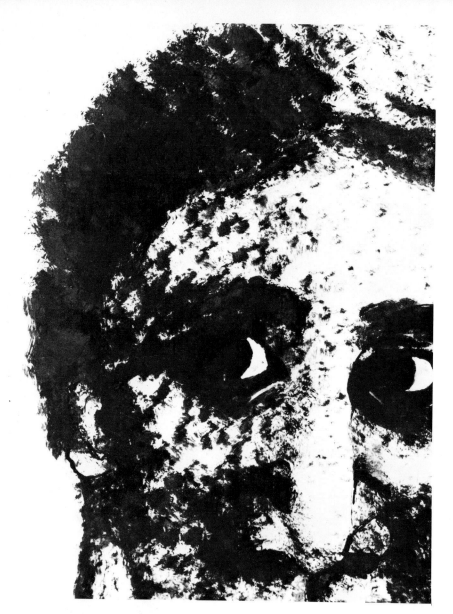

Spattered ink

Squashed brush

Sponge and ink

Detail of a face made by
the use of a brush pressed
against the paper and
twisted with different
amounts of ink on the
brush each time.

A face created by use of ink on a cellulose sponge pressed lightly against paper with ink lines added later.

10.
The Face by Accident

A marvelous way to find a face has always been by accident. In the past the inadvertent discovery of a face on some textured surface, an old wall, a combination of clouds was even formalized by a cult called Tachism.

It is a short step from this serendipity to the calculated attempt to find faces on surfaces that have been prepared for this search. The artist simply creates an opportunity for faces to materialize (with his assistance) on surfaces of random texture or pattern. After spattering, rubbing, staining or otherwise preparing a surface, he looks for ways to link parts of the wash or spots together so that a face starts to form from the combination of these elements.

The crucial question in the evolution of a face by this method is the point at which the artist stops. If he carries the connecting lines beyond the basic force of the original surface, then it may not have the feeling of being discovered. But then, even so, it still has helped him to find a face that probably will not conform to the images he might have utilized if he had started without the stimulus of accident.

Three examples of the techniques for making a surface upon which a face can be drawn are illustrated in this chapter. They include the use of a sponge dipped into ink mixed with water and then lightly touched to the surface of white paper, a brush with the same mixture of ink and water which is squashed straight down upon paper rather than drawn across its surface, and ink spattered from a pen held high above the paper so that it lands on the paper in irregular dots (see preliminary examples below). Each of these, and many more possibilities which can be encouraged by a practice session with the students using rags, feathers, oil and water, wrinkling of the paper, sprays, etc., provides the base for trying to find a face within the random, erratic surface. The face can then be formed either by adding more of the given technique around where a feature is evident until a face begins to form, or by connecting the parts of the surface with other kinds of lines to indicate a face.

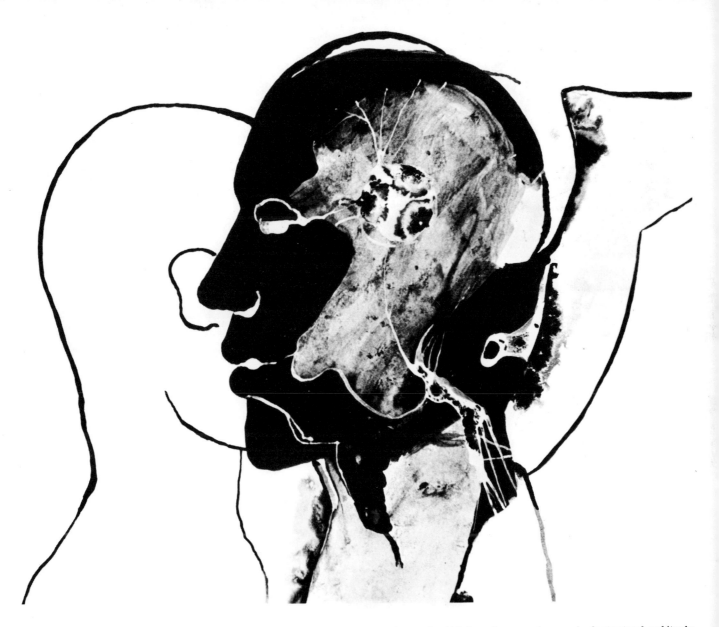

Some of the ways in which the surfaces of these faces were prepared include the use of spattered ink seen on the opposite page and ink touched to wet paper (above). The degree of control in the initial step also varied. In some cases the face was clearly structured, and it only required a bit of line or shadow to complete the face. In others, the surface was pure texture, and the face had to be completely constructed.

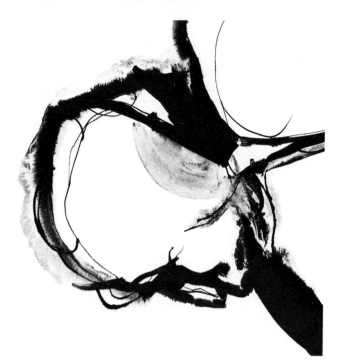

The idea of discovery of the face is the
fortuitous result of using accident as a
stimulus. Now, as shown in these faces,
discovery itself can be played upon. The
faces form out of swirls or emerge from
bold lines as if they were organic — just
a few strokes on a page and a face will
evolve.

A stimulating way to find a face is to draw wild, circular lines that intersect with each other. Then, as in these examples, the challenge is to put a face together between the lines. In drawing the original lines, either hold the drawing instrument so that you have almost no control as to the placement of the lines or actually close your eyes when making them.

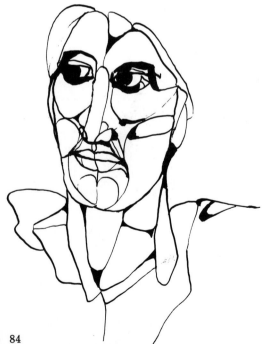

11.
The Face by Washes

Painting the contemporary face involves difficult choices because it may easily lapse into a repeat of faces from the past. There is no harm in some resemblances, but going back to the traditional medium of brush and paint can wipe out much of the new perception already explored.

Therefore, this chapter is called "The Face by Washes" to stress only the technical buildup of the face by layers of paint. Naturally, this is accomplished most easily with water-base paints applied in thin, wet layers. But even more essential than what kind of paint is applied is the sense of tone: tones of washes. Rather than using clear, sharp edges, the students let the parts bleed and run over each other. This tends to support the kinds of accumulated interaction that all the other techniques used thus far have stressed.

There are, naturally, other ways to paint a face in some type of contemporary style besides washes, but this chapter shows work which captures the spirit of the other efforts already explored in being elusive and moving and experimental.

Some procedures with washes are recommended to get the student adapted to the free flow of washes. One approach can be to use wet paper and thinned tempera paint. The water is freely applied to the parts of the face to be painted. Then, while the paper is still very wet, the paint is added. As it starts to dry, slightly thicker layers of paint are introduced, and finally dry and thick paint is used. None of the layers completely covers the others, and the face is only suggested. Only later, when the whole succession of layers has dried, is the face delineated more carefully. It is often successful to have the student do this first with wet paper and ink, which runs more freely, so that he is accustomed to the flow of media. It is also interesting to do the last layer of definition on an overlay of tissue or plastic. Then the rough face beneath can have more than one final face applied over it. In the case of tissue, the most successful final line work can be bonded to the paint washes beneath by brushing acrylic matte medium into the tissue.

A face created with washes may suggest the face as a portion of a larger design (as with the example on the opposite page, reproduced in color on Frontispiece), or it may be like the dripping face on this page. In both cases the face is a flowing, rather than static object. The quality of being in motion is the hallmark of the approach.

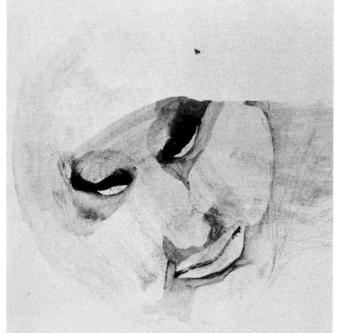

The variety of these types
of washes highlights the
potential of this approach.
Some of the washes are
blended behind clear
forms; some are mixed
with delicate line, and
others evolve into forms.

The block constructions on this and the opposite page were made by cutting out images of faces, pasting them onto cubes, and variously arranging the cubes.

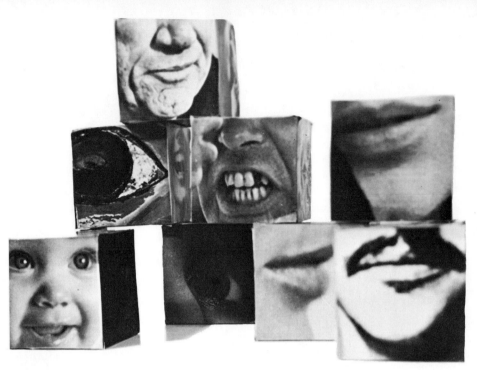

12.
The Face Collected

A face collected is many things. Firstly, it is the putting together of more than one face to produce the contrasting effect of a single face and many at the same time. The parts of faces and whole faces attached to boxes reproduced on this and the opposite page show an approach to this method. It is illustrated in a variety of ways in this chapter — all to give the impact of faces together: composed together, squeezed together, organically reproducing the same faces.

Another aspect of the collected face is the face with its collected parts: that is, with the parts of its setting or background that have not been related to it thus far in previous chapters. Only a few examples of these associated parts are presented, but they serve to place the contemporary face in a slightly broader context. This environmental connection may illuminate more of the significance of trying to establish the identity of the contemporary face.

In order to do a project of the collected face, students can start by cutting a great number of faces from magazines. Then they can make simple cubes by means of cutting and folding paper. On the outside of each cube they can glue the assorted faces — or parts of them.

Finally, if the resources are available, it is worthwhile to have the students move the cubes into different patterns and take photographs of them. The results produce interesting prints and demonstrate the intrinsic value of combining different faces to make a collected image of the face.

An alternate idea for the collected face is to draw a full scene or figure except for the face and then very lightly indicate the face, or even leave the face area blank. The richness of the technique or style of the rest of the picture will seep into the small face area, which then becomes a collection of the things around it.

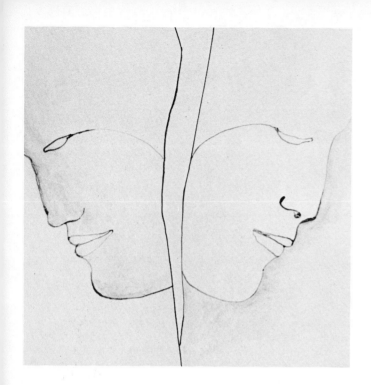

The collected face can be the face
separated and then collected back together
in a cube, back to back or in rows. In any
event, it is the piecing together of it with
the resulting impression of more than one
face, which gives it a collected quality.

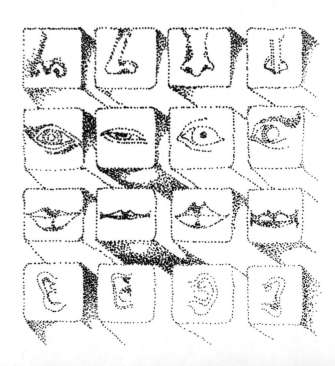

A face is also an empty
space occupying the place
where a face should be. If
the context is
contemporary, then the
face is contemporary —
even without being
delineated.

The figure is an extension of the face. If the student has a feeling for the contemporary power and flow of a face, then it can be suitably extended to the whole figure.

When all of the truths of man — as identified in the depictions of his contemporary face — are assembled, then we must be prepared to acknowledge the meaning of these images. Man makes his own face, and once it is made, must wear it.